BATTLES OF
1942

From El Alamein to Stalingrad

HISTORY ENCOUNTERS

HISTORY ENCOUNTERS

Battles of 1942

First edition

This book was professionally typeset on Reedsy.
Find out more at reedsy.com

Contents

Preview Introduction   iv

Chapter One: Introduction   1

Chapter Two: Malta and Bataan   4

Chapter Three: Battle of Midway   9

Chapter Four: The Battle of El Alamein   14

Chapter Five: The Battle of Singapore   19

Chapter Six: Battle of the Java Sea   23

Chapter Seven: The Battle of the Coral Sea   27

Chapter Eight: The Battle of Dieppe   31

Chapter Nine: Stalingrad The Turning Point   34

Chapter Ten: Pulling all the threads together   37

Discussion Questions 1   41

Discussion Questions 2   42

Discussion Questions 3   43

Discussion Questions 4   44

Discussion Questions 5   45

Discussion Questions 6   46

Discussion Questions 7   47

Discussion Questions 8   48

True or False Questions   49

True or False Answer   51

Conclusion   52

Bibliography (Works Cited)   55

Preview Introduction

A number of major battles in the Second World War were fought by Allied and Axis armies. Among the most crucial of these was the Battle of Stalingrad, the Battle of El Alamein, the Battle of the Coral Sea, and the Battle of Midway.

The Battle of Midway was a definitive victory for the US Navy. The Battle of Stalingrad was a crucial victory for the Russians, forcing the Germans to withdraw and run away. The Battle of the Coral Sea was a significant victory for the Allies, preventing Japan from progressing into the Pacific. The Battle of El Alamein was a conclusive victory for the British, finally driving the Germans out of North Africa. These and other important battles indicated the beginning of the end for the Axis powers.

Chapter One: Introduction

❧

All of us remember learning about WWII at school. Hundreds of books and movies have been written about that terrible war that impacted so many millions and changed the face of the globe and the dynamics between nations. Battles like El Alamein and the siege of Stalingrad are names we all know, but how much detail do we really know about the battles and 1942? Let's have a closer look at them and the experiences of those who suffered through them.

World War II, or WWII, which is also remembered as the Second World War, was a war that involved many countries in Europe and Asia, Great Britain and her colonies, and the USA. The war lasted from 1939 to 1945. It included most of the world's nations, ultimately forming two antagonistic military alliances. On one side were the Allies, which included Great Britain, France, Russia, and, later, the USA; on the other were the Axis powers, Germany, Italy, Japan, and some of the Baltic states. The nations were all in a state of total war for the period, and the war directly involved more than 100 million active participants from more than thirty countries. The main players in the war threw their whole scientific, industrial, and economic capacities behind the war effort, clouding the distinction between military and civilian reserves. Airplanes played a crucial role in the war, including the strategic bombing of public areas. The bombs used to annihilate Hiroshima and Nagasaki were the only nuclear weapons ever used in war.

World War II was the most lethal war in human annals, resulting in 70 to 85 million fatalities. More civilians than soldiers were killed. Tens of millions of humans perished due to genocide which included the Holocaust, death from starvation, including premeditated starvation, the slaughter of groupings of citizens, and disease. In the aftermath of the Axis defeat, the Allied victors invaded and occupied Germany and Japan. War crimes courts were held to judge and punish German and Japanese commanders and leadership.

1942 was an important year in the War because it saw the turning of the tide toward Allied victory, although there was still a long way to go. The attack by Japan on Pearl Harbor in December 1941 forced the US to enter the war, ultimately proving to be a game changer for the Allied forces. The Battle of Stalingrad, which also took place in 1942, offered a crippling blow to Germany, which found itself unable to sustain the war on both the Eastern and Western fronts.

The Battle of El Alamein was also of strategic importance as it struck a decisive blow on the German and Italian war in North Africa.

The battle of Dieppe that same year did not go the way of the Allies and devastated the Canadian forces. However, the battles of 1942 saw a definite shift toward Allied victory even though the war still had 3 long years to go.

Chapter Two: Malta and Bataan

We'll start our exploration of the Battles of 1942 by
looking at the siege of Malta and the battle of
Bataan, the battle of Midway, and the famous battle
of El Alamein.

The Supermarine Spitfire

In 1942, the British amassed huge flotillas of warships to accompany Malta convoys and sent speedy warships to make solo trips to Malta. They also organized "Magic Carpet" supply missions by submarine. Supermarine Spitfire fighters and Hawker Hurricanes were flown to Malta from Gibraltar from aircraft carriers on "Club Runs". The club runs, and Magic Carpets were slang terms for these operations.

Two important battles occurred early in 1942. Malta was an intensive air strike, and Bataan was a ruthless attack ending in the infamous Death March of Bataan.

In 1942, the British amassed huge flotillas of warships to accompany Malta convoys and sent speedy warships to make solo trips to Malta. They also organized "Magic Carpet" supply missions by submarine. Supermarine Spitfire fighters and

Hawker Hurricanes were flown to Malta from Gibraltar from airplane carriers on "Club Runs." The club runs, and Magic Carpets were slang terms for these operations.

Malta was crucial to the Allied war struggle as it furnished a base to interrupt the Axis supply chains to Libya. They also needed Malta to supply the British troops in Egypt. The German and Italian commanders also realized the threat of a Great British stronghold near Italy.

On 20 March 1942, the German forces began an intensive aerial attack on Malta. More than 800 Axis Air Force aircraft were pitted against 140 airplanes protecting the Island of Malta. By the middle of the year, the Axis air assaults on the island and their supply transport neutralized Malta as a war base. An Axis invasion, Operation Hercules (Unternehmen Herkules), was set for July but was aborted. The George Cross was awarded to the citizens of Malta for their bravery under attack.

The siege against Malta lessened after the Allied gained a significant victory at the Second Battle of El Alamein at the end of 1942.

The Battle of Bataan

On 9 April 1942, the Allied troops at Bataan surrendered, and the Philippines fell to Japan. As a result, 78,000 American and Filipino prisoners of war were forced to walk the Bataan Death March, which was 65 miles of pure torture.

The Battle of Bataan was fought between January 7 and April 9, 1942, between the United States of America and the Philippine Commonwealth against the Japanese forces. This battle characterized the most severe stage of the Japanese attack on the Philippines. In January 1942, the Imperial Japanese Army and Navy battalions occupied Luzon and several other islands in the Philippine Archipelago subsequent to the Pearl Harbor bombing of the American navy base.

General Douglas MacArthur merged all of his Luzon-based battalions on the Bataan Peninsula to battle against the Japanese forces. By this time, however, the Japanese were in control of nearly the entire Southeast Asia. The Bataan Peninsula and an island called Corregidor were the Allied strongholds still remaining in the region.

Despite the scarcity of supplies, Filipino and American forces were able to battle the Japanese for some months, engaging the Japanese originally in a fighting retreat to the south. As the combined Allied forces made their last stand, the wait cost the Japanese precious time and staved off immediate victory for Japan across the Pacific. The Americans surrendered at Bataan to the Japanese. The 76,000 soldiers who surrendered in the Philippines were the biggest in Filipino and American military histories and were the biggest United States capitulation since the American Civil War. Soon after surrendering, American and Filipino prisoners of war were compelled to walk the terrible route called the Bataan Death March.

The Bataan Death March

The Bataan Death March began three months after the Battle of Bataan and forced 60,000-80,000 American and Filipino prisoners of war to trudge through the Philippine jungles. The route was only about 65 miles long, stretching from the peninsula to the inland, but the conditions were terrible. The Bataan Death March was one of the tragedies of the War. The Japanese were well known for the harsh treatment of POWs; this was no exception. The prisoners of war were compelled to march through equatorial conditions, undergoing extreme heat, high humidity, and torrential rain without sufficient medical care or concern for their weakened condition going into the march. They endured starvation and had to sleep rough in the severe Philippines jungle. The prisoners unable to keep up the pace were whipped or executed by beheading. A soldier who fell to the ground was immediately shot. Of the 18 000 soldiers who walked to Bataan, approximately 1700 died en route, most Filipinos. The Bataan Death March was devastating for the Filipinos, who suffered disproportionately. The US troops were better treated because the Japanese were more concerned about the ramifications of upsetting America, which might retaliate.

Chapter Three: Battle of Midway

1942 was a busy year for WWII, with the war for world supremacy being fought on many fronts. Hitler was very busy in Eastern Europe and North Africa. The odds seemed to be in Germany's favor. On 10 June, at the massacre of Lidice, the entire Czechoslovakian village ceased to exist, under direct command from Hitler, in retaliation for the death of a senior commander. Eighty-eight children were among the victims.

On 21 June, the Libyan city of Tobruk was occupied by Rommel's Panzer Army Africa. Winston Churchill was enraged, calling the loss a "disgrace." A shockingly high number of Allied troops surrendered, 35000 of them. Rommel was promoted to field marshal.

In Southeast Asia, on 28 June, 7,000 soldiers from the 8th Army were captured by Japanese forces.

The Midway Memorial

The Battle of Midway from 4 to 7 June was a decisive naval battle between the US navy and the Japanese navy. This battle was a significant turning point in the Southeast Asian war. It was a major victory for the USA over the Imperial Japanese forces.

Meantime, the Battle of Midway from 4 to 7 June was a decisive naval battle between the US and Japanese navies. This battle was a significant turning point in the Southeast Asian war. It was a major victory for the USA over the Imperial Japanese forces. Early at the daybreak of 4 June, airplanes from four Japanese navy aircraft carriers bombed and severely weakened the US naval base on Midway. Unknown to the Japanese; however, the US transportation forces were just off the island east and ready to engage them in battle. After the preliminary attacks, the Japanese airplanes attempted to return to their transportation to refuel and rearm. While the airplanes were retreating, the Japanese naval command became conscious of US naval squadrons in the area.

They did not understand that the US Navy could predict and thwart the Japanese onslaught on Midway because they managed to gain intelligence from Japanese codes that their cryptanalysts or code breakers could break. The U.S. Navy succeeded in sinking four Japanese aircraft carriers. The U.S. also took high losses of one aircraft carrier, a destroyer, and 150 airplanes.

Dauntless Dive bombers and Devastator torpedo-bombers from the USS Hornet, USS Enterprise, and the USS Yorktown bombed the Japanese fleet. The Japanese carriers Kaga, Akagi, and Soryu were struck, set alight, and evacuated. Hiryu, the only Japanese carrier which survived, answered back with two tides of attacks, bombing the USS Yorktown, which was seriously damaged but nonetheless afloat, although it was later sunk by a Japanese submarine. Late on June 4, a USS Yorktown patrol plane tracked down the Hiryu, and the Enterprise dispatched dive-bombers to strike it. That raid left the Hiryu on fire and helpless before it sank.

Cryptanalysts

Unbeknownst to Japan, however, American cryptanalysts—code breakers—had cracked Japan's communication codes. When the battle started, United States forces were ready for it. Japan suffered heavy losses as a consequence and spent the remainder of the war on the defensive.

This breaking of the code was extremely helpful. In those days, the codes were fairly simple, but it still took great skill to break them. The US was conscious that the Japanese were intending to launch an onslaught on their armaments in the Pacific. They knew the location was code-named "AF" by the Japanese intelligence because the Navy cryptanalysts had started breaking their communication codes early in 1942. The attack site and the planned time were verified when the US base at Midway gave out a fake message that it was running low on fresh water. Japanese intelligence sent a statement within their intelligence that "AF" was low on fresh water. This confirmed the US intelligence realization that the setting for the attack was the Midway naval base. Station Hypo in Hawaii, the seat of US intelligence in the area, was also able to provide the date of 4 or 5 June and the Imperial Japanese Navy's official order to attack.

The skills of code breakers in 1942 went a long way to helping the allies ultimately win. In fact, codebreaking during world war two was a major skill of the Allies. The Allies used various techniques to break the codes of the enemy. This included using cryptanalysis, which included analyzing letter frequencies and patterns in encrypted statements. The Allies also used sophisticated devices such as the "Enigma Machine," which was used to interpret German codes. Besides this, the Allies used spies and double agents to collect data and information about enemy ciphers and codes. All of these combined techniques assisted the Allies in increasing their advantage in the war and eventually led to their success.

Chapter Four: The Battle of El Alamein

❦

The Battle of El Alamein was an important battle of World War II. It took place in Egypt between 23 October and 4 November 1942. It was the initial main Allied victory against the enemy Axis powers in the campaign in North Africa and is deemed one of the turning points in the war. The battle was between the British Eighth Army commanded by General Bernard Montgomery and the German forces under General Erwin Rommel. After a procession of costly battles, the British troops broke through Axis lines and advanced on the seaport of El Alamein, compelling Rommel to retreat into the desert. The battle caused over 30,000 Allied fatalities and casualties and an approximate Axis casualty total of 40,000.

A Backdrop of Dust and Smoke
*The Battle of El Alamein was an important battle of World War II.
It took place in Egypt between 23 October and 4 November 1942. It
was the initial main Allied victory against the enemy Axis powers in
the campaign in North Africa and is deemed one of the turning
points in the war.*

E l-Alamein is an attractive coastal city in northwestern
Egypt, about 100 km (60 miles) to the west of the
famous city of Alexandria. This was the idyllic site

15

of two important battles between Britain and the Axis forces, Germany and Italy, in 1942. El-Alamein is strategically placed at the northern end of a wide bottleneck, flanked to the south by the impassable and impenetrable Qattara Depression. This critical east-west passageway became an essential defense line held by the British forces and was the furthest point that the German forces had penetrated into Egypt, intent on capturing the Suez Canal.

After the British forces had severely defeated the Italian armies in North Africa, the German commander General Rommel was appointed as leader of Axis troops in Libya. In January 1942, his armies started a fresh push to the east along the North African coast to occupy the strategic Suez Canal. Although they lost Banghāzī earlier in January, the British managed to hold the Germans' lines until May. After this, the German and Italian armies destroyed almost the entire British tank force, took Tobruk, and moved east into Egypt. They reached the British defense line at El-Alamein, now called Al-ʿAlamayn, on 30 June 1942. Rommel struck this line on 1 July, but the following day the British high commander, General Auchinleck, counterattacked, and a typical frustrating battle of attrition evolved. By the middle of July, Rommel was still at El-Alamein, blocked and unable to invade Egypt and seize the Suez canal. The battle was basically a stalemate. In the next battle of El Alamein, in July 1942, however, Rommel was comprehensively beaten.

During this first battle, some 13,250 Allied soldiers were killed or wounded, while the Axis powers suffered about 10,000 casualties.

The Second Battle of El-Alamein

After the first battle of El-Alamein, Bernard Montgomery took command of the British Eighth Army. Since Rommel was on the defensive, "Monty" took this opportunity to amass a sizable force to prepare for the second offensive on El-Alamein.

Because of the Qattara Depression, the Germans could not use their best-moving Panzas, their preferred battle method. The British, however, had their strength in infantry and artillery formations.

By the middle of October 1942, Montgomery could release roughly double the number of tanks and soldiers that Rommel's German-Italian battalions had. The British also had the valuable benefit of air supremacy over the battlefield. Conscious that an onslaught was coming, Rommel prepared for battle as best he could, planting hundreds of thousands of anti-personnel, anti-tank, and mines along the front to hinder the British advance. Rommel was forced by illness to return to Germany just before the battle, which might have affected the outcome.

"Monty" planned a diversionary assault on the south, led by "Free French troops," while the major attack would come from the north close to the coast. The British forces would then smash their way into Axis lines and compel them to counterattack. In this way, the British would erode the German offensive ability.

On 23 October, after dark, a bombardment from 800 guns

broadcasted that the attack was beginning. British sappers, tanks, and infantry progressed quickly to clear the roads through the minefields. Although the German command was taken aback by the violent assault, they launched an intense assault in return.

It seemed, for a period, that the Axis troops might halt the British offensive. The minefields and anti-tank artillery attack knocked out many British tanks. However, the infantry progressed, especially the New Zealand and Australian Divisions, and made it possible for the British army to penetrate Axis offenses. On 2 November, Rommel advised Hitler that they had lost the battle. Although he was refused authorization to retreat, Rommel started withdrawing the German battalions while their Italian allies, who had no motor transport, were left for the British to mop up. Although the German forces were in full retreat, the British were sluggish about following up, so Rommel's army escaped unscathed, but this was not of major importance. This was proved on 8 November during Operation Torch when the Anglo-American forces could land freely in North Africa, paving the way for the end of the Axis footprint in North Africa

Chapter Five: The Battle of Singapore

This battle began on the 8 February and ended on the 15th. After a mere 7 days, the supposedly "Impregnable Fortress" of Singapore surrendered to the Japanese forces. Winston Churchill described this as the "worst disaster" and "largest capitulation" in the history of Britain. At least 80,000 Commonwealth soldiers were taken as prisoners of war.

Leave no man behind

The Bataan Death March began three months after the Battle of Bataan, and it forced 60,000-80,000 American and Filipino prisoners of war to trudge through the Philippine jungles. The route was only about 65 miles long, stretching from the peninsula to the inland, but the conditions were terrible. The Bataan Death March was one of the tragedies of the War. The Japanese were well known for the harsh treatment of POWs; this was no exception.

The fall of Singapore, that beautiful island off the coast of Malaysia, was also called the Battle of Singapore. It took place in the dramatic theater of Southeast Asia during the Pacific War. The Japanese Imperial forces occupied Singapore's British colony, their stronghold in the area. The fighting lasted a mere 7 days. Southeast Asia's main British naval and military base and strategic economic port was

Singapore. It had been of tremendous significance to the British interwar defense protocols. Not only was the loss a strategic disaster, but it was a huge embarrassment, as the capture of Singapore was the biggest British surrender in the long history of the great nation. There were significant casualties, with 1714 killed and double that injured, but the most significant number was the 80 000 taken as prisoners of war

Previous to the skirmish, the Japanese General Tomoyuki Yamashita had progressed with approximately 30,000 soldiers down the Malayan Peninsula. The British mistakenly deemed the jungle terrain impassable, leading to a rapid Japanese advance that outflanked the Allied defenses. British Lieutenant-General, Arthur Percival, was the commander of 85,000 Allied soldiers at Singapore, although multiple units were inexperienced and under-strength. The British outnumbered the Japanese but were vulnerable as much of the freshwater for the island was brought out from storage dams on the mainland. The British demolished the causeway, forcing the Japanese to make an improvised crossing of the Johor Strait. Because Singapore was deemed to be strategically so crucial that Winston Churchill commanded Percival to fight till there were no soldiers left standing.

On 8 February, the Japanese struck the most vulnerable part of the defenses and created a beachhead. Percival had anticipated their crossing from the north and neglected to strengthen the few defenders in time. Information and leadership oversights plagued the Allies, especially as there were limited defensive positions or armament reserves near the beachhead. The Japanese continued to advance, and the Allies ran out of essential supplies. By 15 February, approximately a million civilians in the city were jammed into the only tiny area still held by Allied armies. Japanese aircraft continued to bomb the civilian water reserve, which was anticipated to fail almost immediately. However, the Japanese were also low on supplies, and Yamashita wished to avoid fighting from house to house.

Surrender

Yamashita demanded, for the second time, that they surrender unconditionally, and that same afternoon, Percival gave in. About 80,000 British, Australian, Indian, and Singaporean troops came to be prisoners of war. They joined the 50,000 prisoners taken in Malaya, and many died of abuse, neglect, or forced labor. A few days after the British surrendered, the Japanese started the "Sook Ching purge" and killed thousands of civilians. The Japanese held onto Singapore until the war ended. About 40,000 Indian conscripts from the Indian National Army fought alongside the Japanese forces in the campaign for Burma. Churchill named it the worst catastrophe in the history of the British military. The Sinking of Repulse and Prince of Wales after the Japanese landed in Malaya, the ignominious fall of Singapore, and other unfortunate defeats in 1942, seriously undermined British status. This contributed to British colonial rule ending in the area soon after the war.

Chapter Six: Battle of the Java Sea

The Battle of the Java Sea was an important naval skirmish fought between the Allied forces and the Japanese imperial army on 27 February 1942 in the Java Sea, just off the Indonesian coast. The Allies, including British, Dutch, and American forces, attempted to deter the Japanese from occupying the Dutch East Indies. The Japanese successfully sunk four Allied ships and damaged many more. The Allies suffered more than 1,000 losses to the Japanese forces, a few dozen. The fight was the first important naval battle of the Pacific War and was a definitive victory for Japan.

Battles of 1942

German Soldiers Ready for Battle

The Battle of Stalingrad occurred between 23 August and 2 February 1943. It was a crucial battle of World War II in which Nazi Germany and the other Axis powers battled the Soviet Union to control Stalingrad, now called Volgograd, in the southwest of Russia. The battle was a horrible and bloody combat with an estimated toll of two million casualties. It was a major turning point in the war, with the Germans suffering a conclusive defeat and the Soviet Union regaining power over the city.

What caused the Battle of the Java Sea?

The Japanese invasion of the Dutch East Indies developed briskly as their navy advanced from their colony on the Palau Islands and captured various bases in the Philippines, Borneo, and others. The destroyers, cruisers, and air backing from the hordes of fighter planes operating from these captured bases moved south via the Makassar Strait into the Molucca Sea. The only opposition to this invading onslaught was an insignificant force composed of American, Dutch, Australian, and British vintage warships.

On January 23, 1942, four American destroyers fired on an invasion convoy from Japan in the Makassar Strait. On 13 February, the Allied forces battled without success in the Battle of Palembang to deter the Japanese navy from occupying the main oil port of eastern Sumatra. On 19 and 20 February, an Allied battalion struck a blow at the Eastern Invasion Force just off Bali in a battle called the Battle of Badung Strait. Furthermore, on 19 February, the Japanese air force made two air attacks on Darwin, Australia. This rendered Darwin useless as a naval and supply base to aid the war in the East Indies.

The Battle

The opposing fleets spotted each other late on 27 February, closed to the firing range, and opened fire soon after 4 pm. Both sides showed ineffective gun and torpedo abilities during this battle stage.

The Japanese eventually launched two large torpedo salvoes, which consisted of a bombardment of 92 torpedoes but scored only a single hit, which sank the Kortenaer. The Allied forces suffered severe damage while only one Japanese ship limped away, too injured to continue fighting.

The allied fleet turned away to try and recover, but they were too far out of range for their torpedoes to be effective. They zigzagged through the gray water as night approached, trying to escape the Japanese escort group.

Shortly after this, at about 9 pm, the Jupiter ran into a mine, ostensibly led by their own side, and sunk in shallow water. The much weakened Allied fleet engaged with the Japanese at around 11 pm, and two more ships were mortally struck. Only 111 were saved from the two disabled ships. The two remaining ships, commanded to ignore survivors in the ocean, proceeded to Batavia. The Allies were in a sorry state.

The Aftermath

The Battle of the Java Sea stopped the important Allied naval footprint in Southeast Asia. The Dutch fleet was virtually eliminated from Asian waters, and the Netherlands would never recover full power over its colony. The Japanese controlled one of the most significant food-producing areas (Java). By overthrowing the Dutch East Indies, the Japanese gained control of the fourth-biggest oil-producing region in 1940.

The US and Royal Air Force fled to Australia. Dutch troops, supported by the remains of the British army, fought hard for another week. During this campaign, the Japanese killed many Allied POWs and Indonesian sympathizers. Eventually, however, the Japanese won this decisive battle of attrition, and the Allied forces surrendered to the Japanese on 9 March.

Chapter Seven: The Battle of the Coral Sea

❦

The Battle of the Coral Sea was a significant naval battle between Japanese and Allied troops. The battle was fought between 4 and 8 May in the Coral Sea, just off the Australian east coast. It was interesting and unique because it was the first naval skirmish in history where the ships opposing one another never set eyes on each other. This is because pilots and their aircraft conducted all the conflicts. The fight was a strategic achievement for the Allied forces, as it deterred the Japanese from progressing further into the Pacific region and enabled the Allies to achieve top dog position in the Pacific War.

In the Trenches at Stalingrad
The urban location for the battle amplified challenges that would not have been present in a normal battlefield. It meant fighting and gaining territory from house to house, which meant the complication of many civilian casualties. To add to the challenge, both sides desperately needed supplies. This, in itself, cost many thousands of casualties.

The Perspective.

The Battle of the Coral Sea has often been outraged in importance by the Battle of Midway. Nonetheless, the brutal carrier naval battle in May 1942 was strategically significant. This battle marked the end of the arena of Japanese victories in the Pacific War.

By the start of May 1942, the Japanese Empire was celebrating its triumphant preliminary campaigns, which had launched its Pacific war. The Japanese controlled nearly the whole western Pacific basin.

The British had been annihilated in Borneo, Hong Kong, and Malaya in a run that ended with the disgraceful surrender of Singapore. The crucial Port Rabaul, at the point of New Britain, was also lost in February, providing the Japanese with a significant base close to New Guinea and the Solomon Islands. During March, the Dutch forces had been devastated in Sumatra and Java, and their crucial oilfields fell under Japanese command. Batman and Burma had fallen. The picture for the Allied forces in the Pacific was not looking good. Australia was also in shock, realizing that Japan, while unlikely, could invade its sovereign territory. Japan, realizing the strength of her position, decided that the New Guinea town of Port Moresby would suit its ambition with a large airfield, allowing Japanese air power control over the Coral Sea and as far as north Australia. The actual battle was between the fleet carriers of the two warring nations. The US had broken the Japanese codes and steamed off to intercept the warring fleet.

The Battle

It so happened that the two carrier fleets were placed in near proximity to one another without either of them knowing the other was in the region. The scene was now established for the world's very first carrier war. This seems strange to us today, but communications were not as they are now, and the effects of the weather were very capricious. The opposing fleets were like blind men floundering around in an unfamiliar situation. A sudden and violent air battle occurred when they realized what was happening. Fighter planes after fighter planes were launched, the Japanese lost state-of-the-art fleet carriers while the Americans only lost two rather war-weary old craft. The battle became even more furious as both sides took heavy losses, particularly of aircraft. Japan was confident of victory, believing erroneously that the Americans had lost more ships than they had. There was a great deal of confusion, but the Japanese were confident they had suffered a minor defeat.

The Outcome

Time would disclose, however, that the Battle of Coral Sea was a strategic accomplishment for the Allies because it protected Port Moresby. More importantly, it had an enormous impact on the impending battle of Midway, with much of the Japanese fleet damaged. On a strategic note, the battle of the Coral Sea ended Japanese supremacy in the Pacific.

Chapter Eight: The Battle of Dieppe

The Battle of Dieppe happened on 19 August. It was a combined Allied attack on the Dieppe port in France, occupied by German forces. The operation tested different techniques and tactics that could be utilized in the future Allied invasion of German-occupied Europe. The operation was, unfortunately, a catastrophe; The Allied troops endured enormous losses and could not gain the required foothold in German-occupied France. The Allies lost an enormous number of 3,600 men to the 300 lost to the Germans.

The Battle

The Battle began late because of bad weather, which delayed leaving British ports so the soldiers could start their attack on Dieppe. Operation Jubilee, as it was named, lasted less than 10 hours on 19 August. It was an amphibious attack on the German-seized port of Dieppe. This means the attack came from the sea. The Dieppe Raid was the first important Allied landing on the European mainland since the evacuation of Dunkirk in 1940.

More than 6,000 infantry arrived on Dieppe beach. They were supported by 50 tanks and specially trained commando units. The landings were also supported by at least 250 Royal Navy boats and 1,000 Canadian and Royal Air Force planes.

The Germans were aware of the coming attack and were prepared to make the raid an absolute disaster, with very few Allied fighters ever managing to get off the beach.

In about eight hours of combatting, some 3,600 Allied raid party had been slain, wounded, or taken prisoner. Naval casualties were about 550, and no fewer than 100 airplanes were lost.

The raid was particularly significant for the Canadian forces, who made up the bulk of the assault battalions and the bulk of the casualties, including more than 900 deaths.

The invasion was an expensive failure, but because of the failure, they learned how to modify tactics, improve equipment and gather intelligence more effectively. These lessons learned at Dieppe were crucial in guaranteeing the later successes of the D-Day landings, which helped end the war in Europe.

Canadian Heroes

The Canadian soldiers had been in training since 1939 but had seen little action except for the Battle of Hong Kong. Dieppe was their time to really show their mettle, and although it was a disastrous failure, it was fought with enormous courage and dedication.

Two Canadians earned the Victorian Cross Many acts of great courage took place during the Dieppe Raid, and two Canadians would earn the Victoria Cross for color in the face of danger. Lieutenant-Colonel Cecil Merritt led his men safely out of the battle when the retreat was called, and they could escape back to Britain, although he was captured and held prisoner till after the war. Honorary Captain John W. Foote, a chaplain, braved harsh enemy fire for eight hours to carry men to the first aid posts. He then refused to leave for safety, allowing himself to be captured so he could continue to minister to his fellows in the prisoner-of-war camp.

Chapter Nine: Stalingrad The Turning Point

❧

The Battle of Stalingrad occurred between 23 August and 2 February 1943. It was a crucial battle of World War II in which Nazi Germany and the other Axis powers battled the Soviet Union to control Stalingrad, now called Volgograd in the southwest of Russia. The battle was a horrible and bloody combat with an estimated toll of two million casualties. It was a major turning point in the war, with the Germans suffering a conclusive defeat and the Soviet Union regaining power over the city.

The Battle

The Germans chose Stalingrad to attack because of its industrial potential and its proximity to the Volga

River. This would allow German armies to throttle sources of industry and movement of military vehicles and men.

The battle began in August when the German troops began their assault using the 6th and parts of the 4th Army. The onslaught was supported by bombs that demolished much of the beautiful city. As a result of the city's destruction, the essence of the combat altered to urban warfare, and fighters on both sides had to fight in close quarters.

Both sides brought in huge reinforcements, and by November, German armies had succeeded in shoving the Soviet defense back against the Volga River. On 19 November, the trend of the battle altered. Soviet forces undertook an operation that included targeting the more vulnerable German forces, which were defending the sides of the 6th Army. The force of this counterassault was underestimated, and the vulnerable armies were conquered.

During the Soviet counterassault, the Russian forces cut off the 6th Army. Hitler commanded the army to stay in the city and not to attempt to escape. Severe fighting persisted, but finally, the supplies and ammunition of the Axis armies were finished. On 2 February 1943, the remnants of the 6th Army surrendered. Despite enormous losses, the Soviet army succeeded against the German attack. The tide had turned in their war with Germany.

Battle Conditions

The urban location for the battle amplified challenges that would not have been present in a normal battlefield. It meant fighting and gaining territory from house to house, which meant the complication of many civilian casualties. To add to the challenge, both sides desperately needed supplies. This cost thousands of casualties.

The initial bombing by the German forces had made most of the city a pile of rubble. Still, the Soviet fighters turned the devastation into areas of defense. The harsh Russian winter, which was not understood by the Axis forces, also drove them to surrender.

The Battle of Stalingrad was, without question, one of the most lethal battles in the annals of modern warfare. It left approximately 850,000 Axis soldiers dead, missing, or injured, and took the lives of more than a million Soviet soldiers. Numerous civilians were also slain during the battle. The lives of those people who lived through the battle changed dramatically as they tried to survive in a ruined wasteland.

Chapter Ten: Pulling all the threads together

After the Battle Ends

The Battle of Stalingrad was, without question, one of the most lethal battles in the annals of modern warfare. It left approximately 850,000 Axis soldiers dead, missing, or injured, and took the lives of more than a million Soviet soldiers. Numerous civilians were also slain during the battle. The lives of those people who lived through the battle changed dramatically as they tried to survive in a ruined wasteland.

T he battles of 1942 were a crucial turning point in World War II. During this year, the Allies made substantial progress in Europe, the Pacific, and North Africa. The Battle of Midway, which took place in June, was an important victory for the Allied forces because it destroyed the power of Japan's navy in the Pacific and meant the end of Japanese expansionism in the area. In North Africa, the Allies pushed the Axis forces into a retreat and ultimately won against them in October in the Battle of El Alamein. The Soviets stopped the German advance on the eastern front at the Battle of Stalingrad. The tide of the war started to turn in favor of Russia. Although not across the board, the battles of 1942 meant a major direction change in the war, finally leading to Allied victory.

There are many very accurate and fascinating movies, series, and books about the battles of 1942, and even those with a bit of dramatic license can give us a feeling of what it must have been like to participate in those battles.

But for those who are tired of traditional war movies where you know that the British or Americans are sure to win, albeit through dreadful suffering, stream an interesting take on World War Two in Russia, originally written in Russian, of course. The movie is based on a true incident derived from a novel by Vyacheslav Kondratyev.

The movie *1942: Unknown Battle* is set in Rzhev, USSR. After a particularly brutal battle between the Nazis and the Red Army near a tiny village called Ovsyannikova, only fifty percent of the Red Army's battalion survives. They are freezing, starving, and without reinforcements, and the Nazis are encroaching closer and closer when they receive the command to hold the village to the last man.

While trapped in this significant strategic position, the soldiers try to cope with their fears, knowing they have no chance of survival. With the burden of his fighters' lives on his shoulders, their commander confronts the choice between taking his men to a certain death in battle or being executed by court-martial for disobeying orders and saving them. This poignant story is a look at the tragedy played out daily through WWII and gives a specific look into the courage of the Red Army as they fought to overthrow the Nazis in WWII.

"Genre: Drama
   Original Language: Russian
   Director: Igor Kopylov
   Producer: Sergei Shcheglov, Inessa Yurchenko
   Writer: Igor Kopylov
   Release Date (Streaming): Mar 2, 2021
   Runtime: 1h 53m"

What makes any battle important and tragic is that battles affect people, society, and families. An interesting exercise for any of us is to search the records from World War II and other documents from that time to find out if your ancestors had a role to play during this critical time of the history of the world and what their lives were like because of it. By learning about the battles our forefathers faced, we can face our battles and choose which battles to fight.

Discussion Questions 1

～～⚬⚬⚬～～

The Battle of Midway broke the Japanese hold in the Pacific. Explain what happened. What unsuccessful battle leading up to Midway acted as a training ground for Allied forces?

Discussion Questions 2

❧

The Battle of the Coral Seas was a threat to Australia. How was this threat averted? Did the Japanese ever land on Australian soil?

Discussion Questions 3

W hat are the psychological consequences of war? Why do you think people are so warlike? Justify your opinion.

Discussion Questions 4

H ow did the weather in Stalingrad affect the war? Did the Germans cope less well than the Russians? Yes or no?

Discussion Questions 5

❦

W here was the battle for North Africa won? What strategic landscape feature helped to secure that victory? Elaborate

Discussion Questions 6

E xplain what happened at Dieppe. Which nation was badly affected for the first time? Was there any positive outcome at Dieppe?

Discussion Questions 7

❧

Why were the battles of 1942 so important? What did they mean for the rest of the war? Explain your answer.

Discussion Questions 8

‿◦◦◦‿

D o you think mankind has learned anything from the horrors of World War II? Is war ever justified? What do you think?

True or False Questions

1. **True or False.** The Battle for Singapore was an embarrassment for the allies. Winston Churchill was very critical of his forces. It was a rout.
2. **True or False.** The battle of the Java Sea included one of the less well-known Allies. This was Norway. Norway had a territory near Java.
3. **True or False.** The Battle of El Alamein secured the war in North Africa for the Allies. It took power away from Germany and Italy.
4. **True or False.** During the battle of Stalingrad, the German casualties were much higher than the Russian casualties. It was a disaster for Germany. An absolute thrashing.
5. **True or False.** The Battle of the Coral Sea was interesting because it was fought by planes. The aircraft carriers never saw one another. It was the only battle ever fought like this.
6. **True or False.** The Battle of Dieppe was a defeat for the

Allies. It meant they became fearful of landing on French beaches again. It delayed the progress of the war.

7. **True or False.** The movie 1942: The unknown battle was a fascinating look at the choices in War. It was written in Russian. It was based on a book.

8. **True or False.** The battles of 1942 turned the tide of the war. They gave the edge to the Allies. They gave them hope.

True or False Answer

1. True.
2. False. The country involved was the Netherlands. It was securing its colonies which were part of the Dutch East Indies.
3. True
4. False. Although Germany lost and retreated, the Russian casualties were higher. The battle was a strategic victory for Russia. It was a terrible price to pay.
5. True
6. False. Dieppe acted as a training ground. The Allies learned lessons that gave them courage. It prepared them for the D-Day landings.
7. True.
8. True

Conclusion

The Consequences of War

We've had a fascinating look at the various battles of 1942. We've examined how military supremacy was regained, proving a turning point in Allied fortunes and changing the direction of the war.

However, we've underplayed the effects on human beings: civilians, soldiers, and their families. It doesn't seem right to dwell on the terrible sufferings on the battlefield, drowning in water blazing with fire from oil spills, far from home, the tortures and horror of the forced marches and prisoner of war camps, and the suffering, insecurity, and fear of being an occupied people. But it was real to the people who suffered it, and the consequences carried forward into societies and future generations.

Studies have shown that among the effects of war, the influence on the mental health of civilians is one of the most significant. Studies of the wider population indicate a substantial increase in the prevalence and incidence of mental health problems. Women are affected more often than men, as are vulnerable people like children, the aged, and the disabled. Prevalence percentages correlate with the trauma's extent and victims' ability to access physical and emotional support.

It's many years since WWII ended, with its devastating death toll. Nonetheless, there has been a let up in smaller wars and skirmishes, including the current war between Russia and Ukraine. If you visit nearly fifty years after the end of the Vietnamese war, the population is still terribly emotionally scarred. Then there is Iraq. The ongoing war there has resulted in a generation that has grown up only knowing war.

Wars have had a significant part in the psychiatric narrative in many ways. One legacy of the world wars was the impact of shell shock that left a percentage of soldiers from WWI not eligible for recruitment into the military during the Second World War. This sparked the creation, in the USA, of the "National Institute of Mental Health." How the psychological symptoms manifested among the officers and soldiers helped experts to understand psychiatric responses to stress.

The subject is now widely studied, and research is ongoing for obvious reasons. An example is the 22 nations of the Eastern Mediterranean region. Eighty percent of this population is either in a war situation or has suffered such a circumstance in the last 25 years.

War has a disastrous effect on the well-being and health of countries. Studies show that war situations inflict more death and disability than any disease. War devastates communities and households and disrupts nations' economic and social integrity. The consequences of war include long-term psychological and physical trauma to children and grown-ups and reduced national wealth and stability. Death is a small part of the horror of war. Other consequences are poverty, hunger, disability, economic and social systems failure, and psychosocial disorders. Not to mention the devastating environmental effects and animal suffering.

Maybe it's time for us as a human race to say no to the conflicts that have beset the planet throughout history. It only takes one generation to vote out the warmongers and their greed and rather take their fight for the preservation of the environment and the healing of the planet.

Bibliography (Works Cited)

1. National World War 2 Museum The Battle of Midway. Updated 2023. www.nationalww2museum.org/war/a rticles/battle-midway#:~:text=Breaking%20the%20Cod e&text=The%20attack%20location%20and%20time,was %20the%20base%20at%20Midway.
2. Gilbert A. Battles of El Alamein. Encyclopedia Britannica. Updated 2023 https://www.britannica.com/event/battle s-of-El-Alamein
3. Wikipedia Battle of the Java Sea Updated 2023. https://e n.m.wikipedia.org/wiki/Battle_of_the_Java_Sea
4. Srinivasa Murthy R and Lakshminarayana R World Psychiatry 2006. https://www.ncbi.nlm.nih.gov/pmc/articl es/PMC1472271/
5. Commonwealth War Graves 11 facts about the Dieppe Raid. 2017 https://www.cwgc.org/our-work/news/11-f acts-about-the-dieppe-raid/
6. Limbach R. Britannica. Battle of Stalingrad. Updated 2023

https://www.britannica.com/event/Battle-of-Stalingrad

7. History com Editors. The Battle of Midway begins. Updated 2023 https://www.history.com/this-day-in-hi story/battle-of-midway-begins

Images (License-Free)

T he **Supermarine Spitfire:** In 1942, the British amassed huge flotillas of warships to accompany Malta convoys and sent speedy warships to make solo trips to Malta. They also organized "Magic Carpet" supply missions by submarine. Supermarine Spitfire fighters and Hawker Hurricanes were flown to Malta from Gibraltar from aircraft carriers on "Club Runs". The club runs, and Magic Carpets

were slang terms for these operations. Wikipedia. https://en.w
ikipedia.org/wiki/File:Spitfire_-_Season_Premiere_Airshow_
2018_(cropped).jpg

Leave no man behind: The Bataan Death March began three
months after the Battle of Bataan, and it forced 60,000-80,000
American and Filipino prisoners of war to trudge through the
Philippine jungles. The route was only about 65 miles long,
stretching from the peninsula to the inland, but the conditions
were terrible. The Bataan Death March was one of the tragedies
of the War. The Japanese were well known for the harsh
treatment of POWs; this was no exception. Wikipedia: https://e
n.wikipedia.org/wiki/Bataan_Death_March#/media/File:Pho
tograph_of_American_Prisoners_Using_Improvised_Litters_
to_Carry_Comrades,_05-1942_-_NARA_-_535564.jpg

The Midway Memorial: The Battle of Midway from 4 to 7 June was a decisive naval battle between the US navy and the Japanese navy. This battle was a significant turning point in the Southeast Asian war. It was a major victory for the USA over the Imperial Japanese forces. **Wikipedia. https://en.wikiped ia.org/wiki/Battle_of_Midway#/media/File:Starr_080604 -6331_Unknown_orchidaceae.jpg**

A Backdrop of Dust and Smoke: The Battle of El Alamein was an important battle of World War II. It took place in Egypt between 23 October and 4 November 1942. It was the initial main Allied victory against the enemy Axis powers in the campaign in North Africa and is deemed one of the turning points in the war. Wikipedia: https://en.wikipedia.org/wiki/S econd_Battle_of_El_Alamein#/media/File:El_Alamein_1942_ -_British_infantry.jpg

German Soldiers Ready for Battle: The Battle of Stalingrad occurred between 23 August and 2 February 1943. It was a crucial battle of World War II in which Nazi Germany and the other Axis powers battled the Soviet Union to control Stalingrad, now called Volgograd, in the southwest of Russia. The battle was a horrible and bloody combat with an estimated toll of two million casualties. It was a major turning point in the war, with the Germans suffering a conclusive defeat and the Soviet Union regaining power over the city. Wikipedia. https://en.wikipedia.org/wiki/Battle_of_Stalingrad#/media/F ile:Bundesarchiv_Bild_146-1971-107-40,_Russland,_Kampf_ um_Stalingrad,_Infanterie.jpg

In the Trenches at Stalingrad. The urban location for the battle amplified challenges that would not have been present in a normal battlefield. It meant fighting and gaining territory from house to house, which meant the complication of many civilian casualties. To add to the challenge, both sides desperately needed supplies. This, in itself, cost many thousands of casualties. **Wikipedia. https://en.wikipedia.or g/wiki/Battle_of_Stalingrad#/media/File:62._armata_a_ Stalingrado.jpg**

After the Battle Ends: The Battle of Stalingrad was, without question, one of the most lethal battles in the annals of modern warfare. It left approximately 850,000 Axis soldiers dead, missing, or injured, and took the lives of more than a million Soviet soldiers. Numerous civilians were also slain during the battle. The lives of those people who lived through the battle changed dramatically as they tried to survive in a ruined wasteland. Wikipedia. https://en.wikipedia.org/wiki/Battle_o f_Stalingrad#/media/File:RIAN_archive_602161_Center_of_ Stalingrad_after_liberation.jpg

9 798348 403171